D1607417

BELIEVING IN OURSELVES

BELIEVING IN OURSELVES

The Wisdom of Women

Edited by Susan Feuer

Ariel Books

**Andrews McMeel
Publishing**

Kansas City

ISBN: 0-7407-0444-3

Library of Congress Catalog Card Number: 00-100471

CONTENTS

❧

INTRODUCTION

OUR LIVES ARE
filled with challenges, changes, fulfillment,
surprises, ups, and downs. They are ours, to do
with what we wish, each and every day. When we
are confused or when we take a wrong turn, we
may need some help working through the
muddle, getting back on track. It is during these
times, especially, that we must believe in our-

selves and trust that we can indeed do what we set out to do.

Contained here are nearly four hundred quotations by women, women who all believe in themselves and their talents. Their opinions and feelings—on love, friendship, work, aspirations, knowledge, and more—are voiced within the pages of this book. Through their words, they encourage us to do our best, explore the unknown, fulfill our dreams, and then dream anew. As you read on, you are sure to be inspired. ✺

BELIEVING IN OURSELVES

LIFE'S
RICH JOURNEY

$\mathscr{M}$y favorite thing is to go where I've
never been.

❧

Diane Arbus

That is what learning is.
You suddenly understand
something you've understood
all your life, but in a new way.

❧

Doris Lessing

$\mathcal{B}$ut the whole point
of liberation is that you get
out. Restructure your life.
Act by yourself.

Jane Fonda

*L*ife is what we make it,
always has been,
always will be.

❧

Grandma Moses

*O*ne is not born a woman,

one becomes one.

❦

Simone de Beauvoir

The great thing about getting older is that you don't lose all the other ages you've been.

Madeleine L'Engle

*H*umor is such a strong weapon, such a strong answer. Women have to make jokes about themselves, laugh about themselves, because they have nothing to lose.

Agnes Varda

I could not, at any age, be content to take my place in a corner by the fireside and simply look on. Life was meant to be lived. Curiosity must be kept alive. The fatal thing is the rejection. One must never, for whatever reason, turn his back on life.

Eleanor Roosevelt

There are for starters, grandeur and silence, pure water and clean air. There is also the gift of distance . . . the chance to stand away from relationships and daily ritual . . . and the gift of energy. Wilderness infuses us with its own special brand of energy. I remember lying by the Snake River in Idaho once and becoming aware I could not sleep . . . nature's forces had me in hand. I was engulfed by a dance of ions and atoms. My body was responding to the pervasive pull of the moon.

Lynn Thomas

I like living. I have sometimes been wildly, despair-
ingly, acutely miserable, wracked with
sorrow, but through it all I still
know quite certainly that just to
be alive is a grand thing.

Agatha Christie

She knew what all smart women knew: Laughter made you live better and longer.

❧

Gail Parent

*O*ur way is not soft grass,
it's a mountain path with lots
of rocks. But it goes upwards,
forward, toward the sun.

❦

Dr. Ruth Westheimer

*L*et me stand in my
age with all its waters
flowing round me. If they sometimes
subdue, they must finally upbear me,
for I seek the universal—and
that must be the best.

Margaret Fuller

22

❧

I wanted a perfect ending. . . . Now I've learned, the hard way, that some poems don't rhyme, and some stories don't have a clear beginning, middle, and end. Life is about not knowing, having to change, taking the moment and making the best of it, without knowing what's going to happen next. Delicious ambiguity.

Gilda Radner

I hear the singing
of the lives of women,
The clear mystery, the
offering and pride.

❧

Muriel Rukeyser

❧

In the years since I began following the ways of my grandmothers I have come to value the teachings, stories, and daily examples of living which they shared with me. I pity the younger girls of the future who will miss out on meeting some of these fine old women.

Beverly Hungry Wolf

*Y*ou must learn day by
day, year by year, to
broaden your horizon. The more
things you love, the more you are
interested in, the more you enjoy,
the more you are indignant about,
the more you have left when
anything happens.

Ethel Barrymore

*D*on't be afraid your
life will end; be afraid that
it will never begin.

❧

Grace Hansen

While others may argue
about whether the world
ends with a bang or a whimper,
I just want to make sure mine
doesn't end with a whine.

Barbara Gordon

Going into the wilderness
involves the wilderness
within us all. This may be the
deepest value of such an experience,
the recognition of our kinship
with the natural world.

China Galland

I don't want to get to the
end of my life and find
that I just lived the length of it.
I want to have lived the width
of it as well.

Diane Ackerman

Do not follow where the path may lead. Go instead where there is no path and leave a trail.

Muriel Strode

The distance is nothing;
it's only the first step that
is difficult.

Marquise du Deffand

We older women who know we aren't heroines can offer our younger sisters, at the very least, an honest report of what we have learned and how we have grown.

Elizabeth Janeway

People create their own
questions because they're
afraid to look straight. All you have
to do is look straight and see the
road, and when you see it, don't sit
looking at it—walk.

Ayn Rand

The need for change
bulldozed a road down
the center of my mind.

❧

Maya Angelou

I began to have an idea of my life, not as the slow shaping of achievement to fit my preconceived purposes, but as the gradual discovery and growth of a purpose which I did not know.

Joanna Field

Mama exhorted her children at every opportunity to "jump at de sun." We might not land on the sun, but at least we would get off the ground.

Zora Neale Hurston

If I had to live my life again, I'd make the same mistakes, only sooner.

❧

Tallulah Bankhead

Everybody knows if you are
too careful you are so
occupied in being careful that you
are sure to stumble over something.

Gertrude Stein

Too many wish
to be happy before
becoming wise.

❧

*Susanne
Curchod Necker*

*A*ge puzzles me. I thought it was a quiet time. My seventies were interesting and fairly serene, but my eighties are passionate. I grow more intense as I age.

Florida Scott-Maxwell

*W*hat matters most
is that we learn from living.

❧

Doris Lessing

I soon realized that no journey carries one far unless, as it extends into the world around us, it goes an equal distance into the world within.

Lillian Smith

*L*ife loves to be taken
by the lapel and be told:
"I am with you, kid. Let's go."

❧

Maya Angelou

$\mathcal{E}$very time I think
that I'm getting old, and
gradually going to the grave,
something else happens.

❧

Lillian Carter

You must not think
that I feel, in spite of
it having ended in such defeat, that
my "life has been wasted" here, or
that I would exchange it with that
of anyone I know.

Isak Dinesen

*W*hat a lovely surprise
to discover how unlonely
being alone can be.

❧

Ellen Burstyn

She would not exchange
her solitude for anything.
Never again to be forced to move
to the rhythms of others.

Tillie Olsen

I have fought and kicked and fasted and prayed and cursed and cried myself to the point of existing. It has been like being born again, literally. Just *knowing* has meant everything to me. Knowing has pushed me out into the world, into college, into places, into people.

Alice Walker

It is sad to grow old
but nice to ripen.

❦

Brigitte Bardot

50

*A*ge is not a handicap.
Age is nothing but a number.
It is how you use it.

❧

Ethel Payne

*I*nside myself is a place
where I live alone and that's
where you renew your springs
that never dry up.

❧

Pearl S. Buck

$\mathcal{W}$e are always the
same age inside.

Gertrude Stein

*W*isdom doesn't automatically come with old age. Nothing does—except wrinkles. It's true, some wines improve with age. But only if the grapes were good in the first place.

Abigail Van Buren

The secret of staying younger is to live honestly, eat slowly, and lie about your age.

Lucille Ball

If this was adulthood, the only improvement she could detect in her situation was that now she could eat dessert without eating her vegetables.

Lisa Alther

$\mathcal{A}$nother belief of mine: that everyone else my age is an adult, whereas I am merely in disguise.

❧

Margaret Atwood

*L*ife offstage has
sometimes been a wilderness
of unpredictables in an
unchoreographed world.

❧

Margot Fonteyn

It has begun to occur
to me that life is a stage
I'm going through.

❦

Ellen Goodman

I think I should have no other mortal wants, if I could always have plenty of music. It seems to infuse strength into my limbs and ideas into my brain. Life seems to go on without effort, when I am filled with music.

George Eliot

We learn best to listen
to our own voices if we
are listening at the same time to
other women . . . whose stories, for
all our differences, turn out, if we
listen well, to be our stories also.

Barbara Deming

There is something all
life has in common, and
when I know what it is I
shall know myself.

❧

Jean Craighead George

To be somebody
you must last.

❧

Ruth Gordon

The events in our lives
happen in a sequence
in time, but in their significance
to ourselves, they find their own
order . . . the continuous thread
of revelation.

Eudora Welty

*R*eality is something
you rise above.

❧

Liza Minnelli

When it comes time to do your own life, you either perpetuate your childhood or you stand on it and finally kick it out from under.

Rosellen Brown

*W*hat a commentary on
our civilization, when
being alone is considered suspect;
when one has to apologize for it,
make excuses, hide the fact that one
practices it—like a secret vice!

Anne Morrow Lindbergh

$\mathcal{I}$ believe the second half of one's life is meant to be better than the first half. The first half is finding out how you do it. And the second half is enjoying it.

Frances Lear

*L*ife itself is
the proper binge.

Julia Child

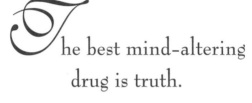

The best mind-altering
drug is truth.

❧

Lily Tomlin

*N*ever economize
on luxuries.

❧

Angela Thirkell

*O*I know what it means to be a miner and a cowboy, and have risked my life when need be, *but*, best of all, I have felt the charm of the glorious freedom, the quick rushing blood, the bounding motion, of the wild life, the joy of the living and of the doing, of the mountain and the plain; I have learned to know and feel some, at least, of the secrets of the Wild Ones.

Grace Seton-Thompson

It is good to have
an end to journey towards;
but it is the journey that
matters in the end.

❧

Ursula K. Le Guin

POINT OF VIEW

There does not have to be powerlessness.
The power is within ourselves.

Faye Wattleton

$\mathcal{I}$ am not belittling the
brave pioneer men, but
the sunbonnet as well as the
sombrero has helped to settle this
glorious land of ours.

Edna Ferber

The best compliment they [men] can give a woman is that she thinks like a man. I say she does not; she thinks like a woman.

Margaret Thatcher

I change myself,
I change the world.

Gloria Anzaldúa

And woman should
stand beside man as the
comrade of his soul, not the
servant of his body.

❧

*Charlotte
Perkins Gilman*

When a man gives his opinion he's a man. When a woman gives her opinion she's a bitch.

❧

Bette Davis

Some memories are realities, and are better than anything that can ever happen to one again.

Willa Cather

*W*hether women are
better than men I cannot
say—but I can say they are
certainly no worse.

❧

Golda Meir

❧

$\mathscr{I}$ am old enough to know that victory is often a thing deferred, and rarely at the summit of courage. . . . What is at the summit of courage, I think, is freedom. The freedom that comes with the knowledge that no earthly thing can break you.

Paula Giddings

It's lucky happenstance
that women's liberation
came along just when it did so that
women can participate in the world
arena and rescue the planet. Just in
the nick of time.

Gretchen Cryer

If you don't like the way the world is, you change it. You have an obligation to change it. You just do it one step at a time.

Marian Wright Edelman

*W*omen are not
inherently passive or peaceful.
We're not inherently anything
but human.

❧

Robin Morgan

$\mathcal{W}$omen are carrying a
new attitude. They've
cast aside the old stereotypes. They
don't believe you have to be ugly or
have big muscles to play sports.

Shirley Johnson

It's better to be a lion
for a day than a sheep
all your life.

❧

Sister Elizabeth Kenny

As a woman, I have
no country. . . . As a woman
my country is the whole world.

❧

Virginia Woolf

Sometimes what we call "memory" and what we call "imagination" are not so easily distinguished.

❧

Leslie Marmon Silko

*L*ike all people
who have nothing,
I lived on dreams.

❧

Anzia Yezierska

A woman is like
a tea bag. You never know
how strong she is until
she gets into hot water.

❧✿❧

Eleanor Roosevelt

*W*oman must not accept; she must challenge. She must not be awed by that which has been built up around her; she must reverence that woman in her which struggles for expression.

Margaret Sanger

If [women] understood and exercised their power they could remake the world.

❦

Emily Taft Douglas

No one is so eager
to gain new experience as he
who doesn't know how to
make use of the old ones.

Marie von
Ebner-Eschenbach

My only advice is to
stay aware, listen carefully, and
yell for help if you need it.

❧

Judy Blume

The most effective way
to do it, is *to do it.*

❧

Toni Cade Bambara

To believe in something not yet proved and to underwrite it with our lives; it is the only way we can leave the future open.

Lillian Smith

There is no such thing as *can't*, only *won't*. If you're qualified, all it takes is a burning desire to accomplish, to make a change. Go forward, go backward. Whatever it takes! But you can't blame other people or society in general. It all comes from your mind. When we do the impossible we realize we are special people.

Jan Ashford

I live a day at a time. Each day I look for a kernel of excitement. In the morning, I say: "What is my exciting thing for today?" Then, I do the day. Don't ask me about tomorrow.

Barbara Jordan

When you know when to laugh and when to look upon things as too absurd to take seriously, the other person is ashamed to carry through even if he was serious about it.

Eleanor Roosevelt

$\mathcal{D}$oing the best at this
moment puts you in the best
place for the next moment.

❦

Oprah Winfrey

Courageous risks are life
giving, they help you grow,
make you brave and better
than you think you are.

❧❧

Joan L. Curcio

$\mathcal{I}$ have always had
a dread of becoming
a passenger in life.

❧

Queen Margrethe II
of Denmark

You grow up the day
you have your first real
laugh, at yourself.

❦

Ethel Barrymore

One can never pay
in gratitude; one can
only pay "in kind"
somewhere else in life.

❧

Anne Morrow Lindbergh

am not eccentric. It's just
that I am more alive than
most people. I am an unpopular
electric eel set in a pond of goldfish.

Dame Edith Sitwell

Rosiness is not a worse
windowpane than gloomy gray
when viewing the world.

❧

Grace Paley

$\mathscr{I}$ cannot and will not
cut my conscience to fit
this year's fashions.

❧

Lillian Hellman

*Y*ou curl your hair and paint your face.
   Not I:
I am curled by the wind, painted by the sun.

Julia de Burgos

Sainthood is acceptable only in saints.

Pamela
Hansford Johnson

In my early days I was a sepia Hedy Lamarr. Now I'm black and a woman, singing my own way.

❦

Lena Horne

The way I see it, if you want the rainbow, you gotta put up with the rain.

Dolly Parton

The one thing that
doesn't abide by majority rule
is a person's conscience.

❧

Harper Lee

⚜

I could never tell where inspiration begins and impulse leaves off. I suppose the answer is in the outcome. If your hunch proves a good one, you were inspired; if it proves bad, you are guilty of yielding to thoughtless impulse.

Beryl Markham

Insanity is doing the same thing over and over again, but expecting different results.

❧

Rita Mae Brown

To have a reason to get
up in the morning, it is
necessary to possess a guiding
principle. A belief of some kind.
A bumper sticker if you will.

Judith Guest

I argue that we deserve the choice to do whatever we want with our faces and bodies without being punished by an ideology that is using attitudes, economic pressure, and even legal judgments regarding women's appearance to undermine us psychologically and politically.

Naomi Wolf

I learned to make my mind large, as the universe is large, so that there is room for paradoxes.

❧

Maxine Hong Kingston

You've got to take
the initiative and play your
game. . . . Confidence makes
the difference.

❧

Chris Evert

To say something nice about themselves, this is the hardest thing in the world for people to do. They'd rather take their clothes off.

Nancy Friday

I never intended to
become a run-of-the-mill
person.

❧

Barbara Jordan

There was no way for me to understand it at the time, but the talk that filled the kitchen those afternoons was highly functional. It served as therapy, the cheapest kind available to my mother and her friends. . . . But more than therapy, that freewheeling, wide-ranging, exuberant talk functioned as an outlet for the tremendous creative energy they possessed.

Paule Marshall

We're half the people;
we should be half
the Congress.

❧

Jeannette Rankin

It occurred to me when I
was thirteen and wearing
white gloves and Mary Janes and
going to dancing school, that no one
should have to dance backward all
their lives.

Jill Ruckelshaus

The fact is, I can have any experience of life I want. I don't have to choose any one thing or act in any one way to define myself as a woman now. I am one.

Ally Sheedy

*W*omen are repeatedly accused of taking things personally. I cannot see any other honest way of taking them.

❧

Marya Mannes

$\mathcal{W}$e can build upon
foundations anywhere if they
are well and firmly laid.

❧

Ivy Compton-Burnett

have a right to my anger,
and I don't want anybody
telling me I shouldn't be, that it's
not nice to be, and that something's
wrong with me because I get angry.

Maxine Waters

The events in our lives happen in a sequence in time, but in their significance to ourselves, they find their own order . . . the continuous thread of revelation.

Eudora Welty

For a long time the only
time I felt beautiful—
in the sense of being complete as a
woman, as a human being—was
when I was singing.

Leontyne Price

Whenever I have to choose between two evils, I always like to try the one I haven't tried before.

Mae West

I am what I am.
Take it or leave
me alone.

❦

Rosario Morales

I am playing with my Self,
I am playing with the
world's soul, I am the dialogue
between my Self and *el espiritu
del mundo*. I change myself,
I change the world.

Gloria Anzaldúa

One loses many laughs
by not laughing at oneself.

❧

Sara Jeannette Duncan

A mistake is simply
another way of doing things.

❧

Katherine Graham

If you obey all the rules
you miss all the fun.

❧

Katharine Hepburn

I would live in a
communist country
providing I was the Queen.

❧

Stella Adler

*W*hen people ask me
why I am running as a
woman, I always answer,
"What choice do I have?"

❧

Patricia Schroeder

I have bursts of being a lady, but it doesn't last long.

Shelley Winters

$\mathcal{O}$ur humor turns
our anger into a fine art.

❧

Mary Kay Blakely

I base most of
my fashion taste on
what doesn't itch.

❧

Gilda Radner

If only we'd stop trying
to be happy, we could have
a pretty good time.

❧

Edith Wharton

Worry less about what
other people think about
you, and more about what
you think of them.

❧

Fay Weldon

*O*ne of the sad commentaries on the way women are viewed in our society is that we have to fit one category. I have never felt that I had to be in one category.

Faye Wattleton

Adventure is worthwhile in itself.

❧

Amelia Earhart

LOVE, FRIENDSHIP, AND SISTERHOOD

The ultimate lesson all of us have to learn is *unconditional love*, which includes not only others but ourselves as well.

Elisabeth Kübler-Ross

It is the friends
that you can call up
at 4 A.M. that matter.

❧

Marlene Dietrich

There are far too many
men in politics and not
enough elsewhere.

Hermione Gingold

A true conception of the relation of the sexes will not admit of conqueror and conquered; it knows of one great thing; to give of one's self boundlessly, in order to find one's self richer, deeper, better.

Emma Goldman

I am not
afraid to trust
my sisters—not I.

Angelina Grimké

My friends are
my estate.

Emily Dickinson

*O*ld memories are
so empty when they
cannot be shared.

❧

Jewelle Gomez

Sometimes I wonder if men and women suit each other. Perhaps they should live next door and just visit now and then.

Katharine Hepburn

Ultimately, love is
self-approval.

❧

Sondra Ray

Good communication
is stimulating as black
coffee, and just as hard
to sleep after.

❧

Anne Morrow Lindbergh

It seems to me that trying
to live without friends is
like milking a bear to get cream for
your morning coffee. It is a whole
lot of trouble, and then not worth
much after you get it.

Zora Neale Hurston

*E*ven where the affections are not strongly moved by any superior excellence, the companions of our childhood always possess a certain power over our minds which hardly any later friend can obtain.

Mary Shelley

*O*ften intimacies between
women go backwards,
beginning with revelations and
ending up in small talk without
loss of esteem.

Elizabeth Bowen

If I can stop one heart from breaking,
I shall not live in vain:
If I can ease one life the aching,
Or cool one pain,
Or help one fainting robin
Unto his nest again,
I shall not live in vain.

Emily Dickinson

To be one woman, truly, wholly, is to be all women. Tend one garden and you will birth worlds.

❧

Kate Braverman

In my experience, there
is only one motivation,
and that is desire. No reasons
or principles contain it or
stand against it.

Jane Smiley

The sharing of joy, whether
physical, emotional, psychic
or intellectual, forms a bridge
between the sharers which can be the
basis for understanding much of what
is not shared between them, and
lessens the threat of their difference.

Audre Lorde

If I had never met
him I would have dreamed
him into being.

❧

Anzia Yezierska

If it is your time love will track you down like a cruise missile. If you say, "No! I don't want it right now," that's when you'll get it for sure. Love will make a way out of no way. Love is an exploding cigar which we willingly smoke.

Lynda Barry

A man when he is
making up to
anybody can be cordial and gallant
and full of little attentions and
altogether charming. But when a
man is really in love he can't help
looking like a sheep.

Agatha Christie

*Secretly, we wish
anyone we love will think
exactly the way we do.*

❦

Kim Chernin

I truly feel that there are as many ways of loving as there are people in the world and as there are days in the lives of those people.

Mary S. Calderone

The bond between
women is a circle—we are
together within it.

❧

Judy Grahn

Mother and child,
yes, but *sisters* really,
against whatever denies
us all that we are.

❧

Alice Walker

The truth is, friendship
is to me every bit as sacred
and eternal as marriage.

❧

Katherine Mansfield

The only thing to do is
to hug one's friends tight
and do one's job.

Edith Wharton

Sisters stand between
one and life's cruel
circumstances.

❧

Nancy Mitford

Treat your friends as you do your pictures, and place them in their best light.

Jennie Jerome Churchill

She became for me an island of light, fun, wisdom where I could run with my discoveries and torments and hopes at any time of day and find welcome.

May Sarton

I want to love first,
and live incidentally.

❧

Zelda Fitzgerald

*L*ots of people want to ride with you in the limo, but what you want is someone who will take the bus with you when the limo breaks down.

Oprah Winfrey

*W*here there is
great love there are
always miracles.

❦

Willa Cather

There can be no situation in life in which the conversation of my dear sister will not administer some comfort to me.

Lady Mary
Wortley Montagu

I have learned that to have a good friend is the purest of all God's gifts, for it is a love that has no exchange of payment.

Frances Farmer

$\mathcal{P}$ower is the ability
to do good things
for others.

❧

Brooke Astor

The growth of true
friendship may be
a lifelong affair.

❧

Sarah Orne Jewett

$\mathcal{I}$ can trust my
friends. . . . These people
force me to examine myself,
encourage me to grow.

❧

Cher

The only good teachers for you are those friends who love you, who think you are interesting or very important, or wonderfully funny.

Brenda Ueland

Most mothers are
instinctive philosophers.

❦

Harriet Beecher Stowe

Nobody has ever
measured, not even poets,
how much the heart can hold.

❧

Zelda Fitzgerald

CHALLENGES AND ACCOMPLISHMENTS

*W*omen have to summon up courage to
fulfill dormant dreams.

Alice Walker

A woman who is willing to be herself and pursue her own potential runs not so much the risk of loneliness as the challenge of exposure to more interesting men—and people in general.

Lorraine Hansberry

I've dreamt in my life dreams that have stayed with me ever after, and changed my ideas: They've gone through and through me, like wine through water, and altered the color of my mind.

Emily Brontë

$\mathcal{D}$reams are . . .
illustrations from
the book your soul is
writing about you.

❧

Marsha Norman

*I*t is in our idleness, in our dreams, that the submerged truth sometimes comes to the top.

❦

Virginia Woolf

I always wanted to be somebody. If I made it, it's half because I was game enough to take a lot of punishment along the way and half because there were a lot of people who cared enough to help me.

Althea Gibson

*L*ife's under no
obligation to give us
what we expect.

❦

Margaret Mitchell

*H*ow wrong it is for
woman to expect
the man to build the world
she wants, rather than set out
to create it herself.

Anaïs Nin

$\mathscr{I}$ knew someone had to take the first step and I made up my mind not to move.

❧

Rosa Parks

$\mathcal{I}$'m not going to
lie down and let trouble
walk over me.

❦

Ellen Glasgow

If the first woman God ever made was strong enough to turn the world upside down all alone, these women together ought to be able to turn it back, and get it right side up again! And now they is asking to do it, the men better let them.

Sojourner Truth

You have to ask the questions and attempt to find answers, because you're right in the middle of it; they've put you in charge—and during a hurricane, too.

Sheila Ballantyne

The challenges of change are always hard. It is important that we begin to unpack those challenges that confront this nation and realize that we each have a role that requires *us* to change and become more responsible for shaping our own future.

Hillary Rodham Clinton

From a timid, shy girl I
had become a woman
of resolute character, who could
no longer be frightened by the
struggle with troubles.

Anna Dostoevsky

I say if it's going to be done, let's do it. Let's not put it in the hands of fate. Let's not put it in the hands of someone who doesn't know me. I know me best. Then take a breath and go ahead.

Anita Baker

You may have a fresh start any moment you choose, for this thing that we call "failure" is not the falling down, but the staying down.

Mary Pickford

I became more courageous by doing the very things I needed to be courageous for—first, a little, and badly. Then, bit by bit, more and better. Being avidly—sometimes annoyingly—curious and persistent about discovering how others were doing what I wanted to do.

Audre Lorde

I have always been driven by some distant music—a battle hymn no doubt—for I have been at war from the beginning. I've never looked back before. I've never had the time and it has always seemed so dangerous. To look back is to relax one's vigil.

Bette Davis

*W*e must not, in trying to think about how we can make a big difference, ignore the small daily differences we can make which, over time, add up to big differences that we often cannot foresee.

Marian Wright Edelman

Changes are not only possible and predictable, but to deny them is to be an accomplice to one's own unnecessary vegetation.

Gail Sheehy

When you get into a tight place and everything goes against you, till it seems as though you could not hang on a minute longer, never give up then, for that is just the place and time that the tide will turn.

Harriet Beecher Stowe

*L*ife's challenges are not
supposed to paralyze you,
they're supposed to help you
discover who you are.

❧

Bernice Johnson Reagon

207

I am incapable of conceiving infinity, and yet I do not accept finity. I want this adventure that is the context of my life to go on without end.

Simone de Beauvoir

I have not ceased being fearful, but I have ceased to let fear control me. I have accepted fear as a part of life—specifically the fear of change, the fear of the unknown; and I have gone ahead despite the pounding in my heart that says: Turn back, turn back, you'll die if you venture too far.

Erica Jong

Life shrinks or expands in proportion to one's courage.

Anaïs Nin

*B*egin somewhere; you
cannot build a reputation on
what you intend to do.

❧

Liz Smith

The next best thing to winning is losing! At least you've been in the race.

❧

Nellie Hershey Tullis

For me life is a challenge.
And it will be a challenge if
I live to be a hundred or if I
get to be a trillionaire.

❧

Beah Richards

When you make
a world tolerable for
yourself, you make a world
tolerable for others.

❧

Anaïs Nin

*L*ife is change.
Growth is optional.
Choose wisely.

❧

Karen Kaiser Clark

$\mathcal{W}$e don't make mistakes.
We just have learnings.

❧

Anne Wilson Schaef

I have always grown from my problems and challenges, from the things that don't work out—that's when I've really learned.

Carol Burnett

I've never sought success in order to get fame and money; it's the talent and the passion that count in success.

❦

Ingrid Bergman

In the first grade, I already knew the pattern of my life. I didn't know the living of it, but I knew the line. . . . From the first day in school until the day I graduated, everyone gave me one hundred plus in art. Well, where do you go in life? You go to the place where you got one hundred plus.

Louise Nevelson

*N*o life is so hard that
you can't make it easier
by the way you take it.

❧

Ellen Glasgow

$\mathscr{I}$ think these difficult times have helped me to understand better than before how infinitely rich and beautiful life is in every way and that so many things that one goes around worrying about are of no importance whatsoever.

Isak Dinesen

I don't believe in failure.
It is not failure if you
enjoyed the process.

❧

Oprah Winfrey

*O*nce I decide to do something, I can't have people telling me I can't. If there's a roadblock, you jump over it, walk around it, crawl under it.

Kitty Kelley

$\mathscr{I}$ used to want the words
"She tried" on my tombstone.
Now I want "She did it."

❧

Katherine Dunham

Please know that I am aware of the hazards. I want to do it because I want to do it. Women must try to do things as men have tried. When they fail, their failure must be but a challenge to others.

Amelia Earhart

*L*ife is either always a
tightrope or a feather bed.
Give me the tightrope.

Edith Wharton

$\mathcal{I}$f you really want
something you can figure
out how to make it happen.

Cher

I learned . . . that inspiration does not come like a bolt, nor is it kinetic, energetic striving, but it comes into us slowly and quietly and all the time, though we must regularly and every day give it a little chance to start flowing, prime it with a little solitude and idleness.

Brenda Ueland

To think too long
about doing a thing often
becomes its undoing.

❧

Eva Young

I've always believed
that one woman's success
can only help another
woman's success.

❦

Gloria Vanderbilt

*W*e write our own
destiny. We become
what we do.

❧

*Madame Chiang
Kai-Shek*

Gift, like genius,
I often think only means
an infinite capacity
for taking pains.

❧

Jane Ellice Hopkins

You must accept that you might fail; then, if you do your best and still don't win, at least you can be satisfied that you've tried. If you don't accept failure as a possibility, you don't set high goals, you don't branch out, you don't try— you don't take the risk.

Rosalynn Carter

There are two ways of meeting difficulties: You alter the difficulties or you alter yourself to meet them.

❧

Phyllis Bottome

❧

$\mathcal{I}$ looked on child rearing not only as a work of love and duty but as a profession that was fully interesting and challenging as any honorable profession in the world and one that demanded the best that I could bring to it.

Rose Kennedy

The worst part of success
is to try to find someone
who is happy for you.

❧

Bette Midler

Competition is easier to accept if you realize it is not an act of oppression or abrasion. . . . I've worked with my best friends in direct competition.

Diane Sawyer

*D*o not wait for leaders;
do it alone, person to person.

❧

Mother Teresa

*W*omen are always being tested . . . but ultimately, each of us has to define who we are individually and then do the very best job we can to grow into that.

Hillary Rodham Clinton

She had nothing to fall back on; not maleness, not whiteness, not ladyhood, not anything. And out of the profound desolation of her reality she may well have invented herself.

Toni Morrison

Creative minds have
always been known
to survive any kind of
bad training.

❦

Anna Freud

$\mathcal{A}$ life of reaction is
a life of slavery,
intellectually and spiritually.
One must fight for a life of
action, not reaction.

Rita Mae Brown

If we had no winter,
the spring would not be
so pleasant: If we did not sometimes
taste of adversity, prosperity would
not be so welcome.

Anne Bradstreet

I seldom think about my limitations, and they never make me sad. Perhaps there is just a touch of yearning at times; but it is vague, like a breeze among flowers.

Helen Keller

The only courage that
matters is the kind
that gets you from one
moment to the next.

❧

Mignon McLaughlin

*S*ometimes, I feel discriminated against, but it does not make me angry. It merely astonishes me. How *can* any deny themselves the pleasure of my company? It's beyond me.

Zora Neale Hurston

I'll have to, as you say,
take a stand, do some-
thing toward shaking up that system.
. . . Despair . . . is too easy an out.

Paule Marshall

I had reasoned this out in my mind, there was two things I had a right to, liberty and death. If I could not have one, I would have the other, for no man should take me alive.

Harriet Tubman

*F*ate cast me to play the role of an ugly duckling with no promise of swanning. Therefore, I sat down when a mere child—fully realizing just how *utterly* "mere" I was—and figured out my life early. Most people do it, but they do it too late. At any rate, from the beginning I have played my life as a comedy rather than the tragedy many would have made of it.

Marie Dressler

We owe most of our great inventions and most of the achievements of genius to idleness—either enforced or voluntary. The human mind prefers to be spoon-fed with the thoughts of others, but deprived of such nourishment it will, reluctantly, begin to think for itself—and such thinking, remember, is original thinking and may have valuable results.

Agatha Christie

I really do believe I can accomplish a great deal with a big grin. I know some people find that disconcerting, but that doesn't matter.

Beverly Sills

There are some things
you learn best in calm,
and some in storm.

❧

Willa Cather

When in doubt, make a
fool of yourself. There is
a microscopically thin line between
being brilliantly creative and acting
like the most gigantic idiot on earth.
So what the hell, leap!

Cynthia Heimel

I am still learning—how to take joy in all the people I am, how to use all my selves in the service of what I believe, how to accept when I fail and rejoice when I succeed.

Audre Lorde

You can't be brave if
you've only had wonderful
things happen to you.

❧

Mary Tyler Moore

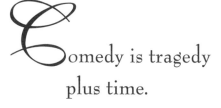

Comedy is tragedy
plus time.

Carol Burnett

One day I found myself saying to myself, "I can't live where I want to. I can't even say what I want to!" I decided I was a very stupid fool not to at least paint as I wanted to.

Georgia O'Keeffe

*S*uccess doesn't come
to you. You go to it.

Marva Collins

*A*rrange whatever
pieces come your way.

❦

Virginia Woolf

To be successful,
the first thing to do is
fall in love with your work.

❧

Sister Mary Lauretta

I long to accomplish a
great and noble task,
but it is my chief duty to
accomplish small tasks as if
they were great and noble.

Helen Keller

*J*ust don't give up trying
to do what you really
want to do. Where there is love
and inspiration, I don't think
you can go wrong.

Ella Fitzgerald

$\mathcal{D}$reams come a size
too big so that we can
grow into them.

Josie Bisset

SELF-ESTEEM

All serious daring starts from within.

Eudora Welty

It was on that road and at that hour that I first became aware of my own self, experienced an inexpressible state of grace, and felt one with the first breath of air that stirred, the first bird, and the sun so newly born that it still looked not quite round.

Colette

Every time you don't
follow your inner
guidance, you feel a loss of
energy, loss of power, a sense
of spiritual deadness.

Shakti Gawain

*L*et the world know you
as you are, not as
you think you should be, because
sooner or later, if you are posing,
you will forget the pose, and
then where are you?

Fanny Brice

267

I'll walk where my own
nature would be leading—
It vexes me to choose
another guide.

❧✦❧

Emily Brontë

Each being is sacred—
meaning that each has
inherent value that cannot be
ranked in a hierarchy or compared
to the value of another being.

Starhawk

am never free of the past.
I have made it crystal clear
that I believe the past is part of
the present which becomes
part of the future.

Lee Krasner

Don't be afraid of the space between your dreams and reality. If you can dream it, you can make it so.

❧

Belva Davis

The future belongs to those who believe in the beauty of their dreams.

❧

Eleanor Roosevelt

I have no regrets. I wouldn't have lived my life the way I did if I was going to worry about what people were going to say.

Ingrid Bergman

love my past. I love my present. I'm not ashamed of what I've had, and I'm not sad because I have it no longer.

Colette

There are people who put their dreams in a little box and say, "Yes, I've got dreams, of course, I've got dreams." Then they put the box away and bring it out once in a while to look in it, and yep, they're still there. These are *great* dreams, but they never even get out of the box. It takes an uncommon amount of guts to put your dreams on the line, to hold them up and say, "How good or how bad am I?" That's where courage comes in.

Erma Bombeck

You need only claim the events of your life to make yourself yours. When you truly possess all you have been and done, which may take some time, you are fierce with reality.

Florida Scott-Maxwell

You have to have
confidence in your ability,
and then be tough enough
to follow through.

Rosalynn Carter

That's the risk you take if
you change: that people
you've been involved with won't like
the new you. But other people who
do will come along.

Lisa Alther

Women are the architects of society.

❧

Harriet Beecher Stowe

Make it a rule of life never to regret and never look back. We all live in suspense, from day to day, from hour to hour; in other words, we are the hero of our own story.

Mary McCarthy

I'm tough, ambitious,
and I know exactly what
I want. If that makes me
a bitch, okay.

❧

Madonna

I am never afraid
of what I know.

❧

Anna Sewell

❧

*N*o coward soul is mine,
No trembler in the world's storm-troubled
sphere:
I see Heaven's glories shine,
And faith shines equal, arming me from fear.

Emily Brontë

Don't compromise
yourself. You are all
you've got.

❧

Janis Joplin

If you think you can,
you can. And if you think
you can't, you're right.

❦

Mary Kay Ash

Asserting yourself
while respecting others is
a very good way to win
respect yourself.

❧

Janice LaRouche

Follow your image
as far as you can no matter
how useless you think it is.
Push yourself.

❧

Nikki Giovanni

*T*here *is* a fountain of
youth: It is your mind,
your talents, the creativity you
bring to your life and the lives
of people you love. When you
learn to tap this source, you will
truly have defeated age.

Sophia Loren

288

Who I am is
the best I can be.

Leontyne Price

Your thorns are the
best part of you.

❧

Marianne Moore

*D*on't shut yourself up in a bandbox because you are a woman, but understand what is going on, and educate yourself to take part in the world's work for it all affects you and yours.

Louisa May Alcott

I will never abdicate.
I shall always want everything.
To accept my life I must
prefer it.

❧❧❧

Marie Lenéru

*A*s one goes through
life one learns that if you
don't paddle your own canoe,
you don't move.

❧

Katharine Hepburn

I will not be just a tourist
in the world of images,
just watching images passing by
which I cannot live in, make love to,
possess as permanent sources of
joy and ecstasy.

Anaïs Nin

I long to put the experience of fifty years at once into your young lives, to give you at once the key to that treasure chamber every gem of which has cost me tears and struggles and prayers, but you must work for these inward treasures yourselves.

Harriet Beecher Stowe

I'm not going to limit myself just because people won't accept the fact that I can do something else.

❧

Dolly Parton

*S*ome of us just go
along . . . until that
marvelous day people stop intimi-
dating us—or should I say we refuse
to let them intimidate us?

Peggy Lee

*L*et me listen to me
and not to them.

❧

Gertrude Stein

We've been taught to respect our fears, but we must learn to respect ourselves and our needs.

❧

Audre Lorde

It is necessary to try
to pass one's self always;
this occupation ought to last
as long as life.

❧

*Queen Christina
of Sweden*

If I had to live my life over again, I'd dare to make more mistakes next time.

Nadine Stair

$\mathcal{I}$ wouldn't give you a dime for my seat in the Senate if I couldn't vote according to my convictions and conscience.

Hattie W. Caraway

In youth we learn;
in age we understand.

❧

*Marie von
Ebner-Eschenbach*

$\mathcal{J}$f you haven't forgiven
yourself something, how
can you forgive others?

❧

Dolores Huerta

We must overcome the notion that we must be regular. . . . It robs you of the chance to be extraordinary and leads you to the mediocre.

Uta Hagen

*M*aybe being
oneself is always
an acquired taste.

❧

Patricia Hampl

Character—the willingness
to accept responsibility
for one's own life—is the source
from which self-respect springs.

Joan Didion

As I grow older, part of my emotional survival plan must be to actively seek inspiration instead of passively waiting for it to find me.

Bebe Moore Campbell

It only takes one person
to change your life—you.

❧

Ruth Casey

I've always been independent, and I don't see how it conflicts with femininity.

❧

Sylvia Porter

We will be victorious
if we have not forgotten
how to learn.

❧

Rosa Luxemburg

We will discover the nature of our particular genius when we stop trying to conform to our own or to other people's models, learn to be ourselves, and allow our natural channel to open.

Shakti Gawain

When I was growing up
I always wanted to be someone.
Now I realize I should have
been more specific.

❧

Lily Tomlin

$\mathcal{L}$ong tresses down to
the floor can be beautiful,
if you have that, but learn
to love what you have.

❧

Anita Baker

You are the product of
your own brainstorm.

❧

*Rosemary
Konner Steinbaum*

Why not be oneself? That is the whole secret of a successful appearance. If one is a greyhound why try to look like a Pekinese?

Dame Edith Sitwell

*L*ove yourself first and everything else falls into line. You really have to love yourself to get anything done in this world.

Lucille Ball

I was raised to sense what someone wanted me to be and be that kind of person. It took me a long time not to judge myself through someone else's eyes.

Sally Field

What I wanted to
be when I grew up
was—in charge.

❦

Wilma Vaught

Friendship with oneself is all important, because without it one cannot be friends with anyone else in the world.

Eleanor Roosevelt

Trust your gut.

Barbara Walters

It is never too
late to be what you
might have been.

George Eliot

$\mathcal{J}$f you do not tell the
truth about yourself
you cannot tell it
about other people.

❦

Virginia Woolf

We have to dare to
be ourselves, however
frightening or strange that
self may prove to be.

❧

May Sarton

I am a woman who
enjoys herself very much;
sometimes I lose,
sometimes I win.

❧

Mata Hari

I was thought to be "stuck-up." I wasn't. I was just sure of myself. This is and always has been an unforgivable quality to the unsure.

Bette Davis

*Just as you inherit
your mother's brown eyes,
you inherit part of yourself.*

❧

Alice Walker

I own my life. And only mine. And so I shall appreciate my person. And so I shall make proper use of myself.

Ruth Beebe Hill

We are the hero of our own story.

❧

Mary McCarthy

I feel that what we must say to one another is based on encouraging each of us to be true to herself: "Now that we are equal, let us dare to be different!"

Maria de Lourdes Pintasilgo

$\mathcal{T}$hink wrongly, if you please, but in all cases think for yourself.

❧

Doris Lessing

WORK
AND CAREER

*W*omen's place is in the House—
and in the Senate.

Gloria Schaffer

Neither woman nor man lives by work, or love, alone. . . . The human self defines itself and grows through love *and* work: All psychology before and after Freud boils down to that.

Betty Friedan

I was brought up to believe that the only thing worth doing was to add to the sum of accurate information in the world.

Margaret Mead

*W*here I was born,
and where and how I
lived is unimportant. It is what I
have done and where I have been
that should be of interest.

Georgia O'Keeffe

*B*e bold. If you're
going to make an error,
make a doozy, and don't be
afraid to hit the ball.

❧

Billie Jean King

I have yet to hear
a man ask for advice on
how to combine marriage
and a career.

❧

Gloria Steinem

$\mathcal{I}$'ve always tried to go a
step past wherever people
expected me to end up.

❧

Beverly Sills

$\mathscr{I}$ never painted dreams.
I painted my own reality.

❧

Frida Kahlo

I look back on my life
like a good day's work,
it was done and I am
satisfied with it.

❧

Grandma Moses

Success is often achieved
by those who don't know
that failure is inevitable.

❧

Coco Chanel

believe in my work and the joy of it. You have to be with the work and the work has to be with you. It absorbs you totally and you absorb it totally. Everything must fall by the wayside by comparison.

Louise Nevelson

I have a brain and a uterus, and I use both.

❧

Patricia Schroeder

A strong woman artist who is not afraid of herself, her sexuality, passion, symbols, language, who is fearless, willing to take any and all risks, often produces work that is staggeringly beautiful and at the same time frightening, dangerous, something to be reckoned with.

Laura Farabough

Women need to see ourselves as individuals capable of creating change. That is what political and economic power is all about: having a voice, being able to shape the future. Women's absence from decision-making positions has deprived the country of a necessary perspective.

Madeleine Kunin

$\mathcal{M}$y passions were all gathered together like fingers that made a fist. Drive is considered aggression today; I knew it then as purpose.

Bette Davis

I don't know everything,
I just do everything.

❧

Toni Morrison

*E*ach story is like a new
challenge or a new
adventure and I don't find help
anywhere, or look for it
anywhere, except inside.

Eudora Welty

*W*hile I can't say there was a particular moment when I attended a concert, heard a piece and was overwhelmed, music was always around, and I just sang for the pleasure of it.

Barbara Hendricks

Whatever you do, don't give up. Because all you can do once you've given up is bitch. I've known some great bitchers in my time. With some it's a passion, with others an art.

Molly Ivins

It's very important to
define success for
yourself. If you really want to
reach for the brass ring, just
remember that there are
sacrifices that go along.

Cathleen Black

I was taught that the way of progress is neither swift nor easy.

❦

Madame Curie

I try to balance my life.
When I'm home, I give
quality time. . . . I'm happy I've
achieved what I have without
losing my head.

Patti LaBelle

I'll stay until I'm tired of it. So long as Britain needs me, I shall never be tired of it.

❧

Margaret Thatcher

We should try to bring to any power what we have as women. We will destroy it all if we try to imitate that absolutely unfeeling, driving ambition that we have seen coming at us across the desk.

Colleen Dewhurst

𝒟uring the month of June I acted as a pony express rider carrying the U.S. mail between Deadwood and Custer, a distance of fifty miles. . . . It was considered the most dangerous route in the Hills, but as my reputation as a rider and quick shot was well known, I was molested very little, for the toll gatherers looked on me as being a good fellow, and they knew that I never missed my mark.

Martha Jane Burke

$\mathcal{I}$ think it's the end of progress if you stand still and think of what you've done in the past. I keep on.

Leslie Caron

None of us suddenly becomes something overnight. The preparations have been in the making for a lifetime.

Gail Godwin

*O*f course I realized there
was a measure of danger.
Obviously I faced the possibility
of not returning when first I
considered going. Once faced and
settled there really wasn't any good
reason to refer to it.

Amelia Earhart

I'm cautious about making money at something that is not the love of my life.

Emily Prager

Unfortunately, there are still many women in the business world who refuse to support women. I call them "Honorary Males"—women who think that power is to be had only in the company of men. Women must realize they have power—economic and political. Don't give your power away; use it for yourself and for the benefit of other women.

Ginger Purdy

$\mathcal{A}$s for me, prizes
mean nothing. My
prize is my work.

❦

Katharine Hepburn

*O*ne only gets to the top
rung on the ladder by
steadily climbing up one at a time,
and suddenly all sorts of powers, all
sorts of abilities . . . become within
your own possibility and you think,
"Well, I'll have a go, too."

Margaret Thatcher

363

If you rest, you rust.

Helen Hayes

Choose to have a career early and a family late. Or choose to have a family early and a career late—but plan a long life.

Dr. Janet Davison Rowley

The secret of joy in work
is contained in one word—
excellence. To know how to do
something well is to enjoy it.

Pearl S. Buck

I've never had a day when I didn't want to work. . . . In my studio I'm as happy as a cow in her stall.

❧

Louise Nevelson

367

I had already learned from more than a decade of political life that I was going to be criticized no matter what I did, so I might as well be criticized for something I wanted to do. (If I had spent all day "pouring tea," I would have been criticized for that too.)

Rosalynn Carter

The penalty of success
is to be bored by people
who used to snub you.

❧

Nancy Astor

I don't care about the Oscar. I make movies to support the causes I believe in, not for any honors. I couldn't care less whether I win an Oscar or not.

Jane Fonda

I see no reason to
keep silent about my
enjoyment of the sound of
my own voice as I work.

❧

Muriel Spark

I've just been so interested in what I was doing [genetic research] that I never thought of stopping.

❧

Barbara McClintock

We can't take any
credit for our talents.
It's how we use them
that counts.

Madeleine L'Engle

This book was typeset in Bernhard Modern, OPTIBauerText, and Shelley Volante Script by Nina Gaskin.

❧

Book design by Judith Stagnitto Abbate